T0158953

THEY CALL ME

MOM

A heartfelt journey through infertility and adoption

JENNY CIOTO

WESTBOW
PRESS®
A DIVISION OF THOMAS NELSON
& ZONDERVAN

WestBow Press books may be ordered through booksellers or by contacting:

WestBow Press
A Division of Thomas Nelson & Zondervan
1663 Liberty Drive
Bloomington, IN 47403
www.westbowpress.com
1 (866) 928-1240

ISBN: 978-1-5127-9615-5 (sc)
ISBN: 978-1-5127-9616-2 (hc)
ISBN: 978-1-5127-9614-8 (e)

Library of Congress Control Number: 2017911233

Print information available on the last page.

WestBow Press rev. date: 7/27/2017

Contents

And anyone who welcomes a little child like this on my behalf is welcoming me.
—Matthew 18:5 (NLT)

1

Mom Is a Noun

*A*m *I even a mom?* Yes, that was the secret question I asked myself the night before my big Momcon conference. *Am I even a mom?* It hurt. I knew I was going to a convention with three thousand other women, other mothers, and I wondered if I would be the only one who had never been pregnant.

I looked up the definition of "mother" because I'm insane. The first definition that came up was from the *Merriam-Webster Dictionary,* "Mother: noun—a woman in relation to a child or children to whom she has given birth."

Wow. That just confirmed my fear. I have five children I love and would give my life for. Yet I have never had the blessing of giving birth. I raise them. I care for them. I teach them about the Lord and manners and how to read. I kiss their boo-boos and hug them good night. They call me Mom, yet biologically we are different.

My journey to motherhood came through a very rough struggle with infertility. The sting of infertility left some unexpected insecurities in me.

Normally, it's no big deal to me. This question of whether I'm a mom never comes up except when I'm in a roomful of mothers of preschoolers, those who are or were recently pregnant, and/or nursing women. They tend to talk about pregnancy a lot and all that comes with. I don't mind talking about it. I've gotten over crying every time someone else is pregnant. I find it sad sometimes, but I've accepted God's role for me. Though not everyone has. Not everyone is nice about it. I've had women ask the most insensitive things.

My favorite thing people say when they find out I've never given birth is, "One day you might have kids of your own." Wow. I just get the air knocked out of me with this one. I want to say something witty back, but I don't. I just nod because there is no right thing to say.

I wondered if that would happen at the conference. Would I be judged? Would they accept me? I confess I never told a soul at Momcon that I did not have my children through pregnancy. I was able to avoid anyone asking me about pregnancy. No one directly asked me, and I kept quiet when the subject came up because I didn't feel comfortable sharing.

Even writing this seems too personal. I started writing this before I went to the conference, and I'm still writing it weeks later. I'm trying to figure out the balance between the right amount to share because it could potentially help someone else, and what is too much.

I Googled the definition of "mother" again. Yes, I'm a glutton for punishment, but I figured there had to be another definition. On Google's drop-down definition, I found "mother: verb—bring up a child with care and affection." I liked that one. I'm that. I am the verb of being a mother.

Can I be a verb? As my teenager informs me, "Mom is a noun. Why are you even looking this up? You're a mom, Mom."

So why do these insecurities come up? My teenager thinks of it so simply. She believes, as do her four younger siblings, that I am her mom. So why do I worry about what society says or thinks? The answer is simple. Because I live in the world. Because I read the newspaper article about a woman and her "adopted daughter" who died in a fire. The article didn't just say daughter; it said "adopted daughter." Why would that matter? Did she raise that child differently? Did she parent one the "biological mothering way" and that one the "adopted mothering way"? Really, people! It's her daughter! I bet that mother loved her. I bet that mother loved her just the same as any other child she had. The media's need to point out who is adopted and who is biological drives me crazy. I'm not sure why they can't just call a son or daughter a son or daughter. Is it really being factual? How do the kids feel about being referred to all the time as the adopted son and daughter?

When Hollywood stars have blended families who have adopted and biological kids, the magazines love to point out who is adopted and who is biological. Why is it necessary to separate them out? They are a family. They operate as a family. I hope and pray that there are not families out there who treat children differently based on if they are biological, step, or adopted. They are children. Treat them right. Raise them as God has entrusted you to.

I'm not sure of God's process when he's making up family dynamics. I feel that no family is made by mistake no matter how they are formed. I guess there are instances where telling a story about being a blended family might be a part of someone's testimony. In talking about how many kids someone has, wouldn't you just give a number, not a rundown? It could be my own insecurities or overprotectiveness coming out, but I never want my kids to *feel* like they're adopted. I want them to just *be* adopted.

Man leaves his father and mother
and is united to his wife,
And the two become one flesh.
—Genesis 2:24 (NIV)

2

The Beginning

L et me start at the beginning of my adventure in becoming a mom. In the summer of 2007, I was a brand-new bride. I was medically retired from the air force one month before I got married. It came as quite a blow to me because the air force had been my identity in my twenties. Now I was looking at being a wife and a stepmom, leaving the world I knew behind. I moved to be with Marc, so I was forty minutes away from my closest friend. It was still a doable drive but lonely on the day-to-day level not getting to see people I knew. Everything was new, and it was scary and a little exciting. I loved my new shake-and-bake family and looked at it as the next adventure.

I call them my shake-and-bake family because they came as a ready-made package. This man I had grown to love had this cute, little six-year-old with blond curls and her dad's blue eyes. This girl grabbed my heart so fast I didn't see it happen. Marc (my husband) was a wonderful father, and I wasn't quite sure where I fit into this new family.

Ashley, my new daughter from another mother, was so curious. She loved learning and playing make-believe. She acted like no stepdaughter I had ever read about or seen in movies. The stepmom is always so mean in any family movie. Have you noticed that? Then the child is always playing pranks or is unhappy with the dad's decision and tries to break up the happy couple. With family movies being my main source of knowledge about stepparenting, I wasn't too sure what to do.

Thankfully, she and I got to know each other. We both realized that we were a perfect fit. I fell in love with this little girl almost as much as I had her dad. Best of all, she loved me too! She thought I was great and did what I asked of her. I thought she was great, and she had me wrapped around her pinky finger.

I introduced her to God and His Son, and she absorbed it all. (Marc was still very early in his walk with Christ and hadn't yet figured out how to teach what he was learning himself.) It's funny the stereotypes we get in our heads because of movies. I expected the brat who tried to undermine me and tie me up in the basement. I expected her to have some pushback about me marrying her dad. I even prepared my ears and heart for her to someday say, "You're not my mom!" It all would have been what I considered normal. She is far from your typical kid though.

All of those stereotypes were dead wrong. There was just this sweet little girl that talked *a lot*. Okay, "she talked a lot" is probably an understatement, but she was my first experience of having a child. I loved it. I may have spoiled her just a bit during my first summer with nothing to do but take care of her and my new husband. It was surreal. Ashley had weekly visitation at her mother's house, which felt like forever. Even though I got to see her all day long, that separation at night felt horrible. However, it gave Marc and me time to be newlyweds together, which was fun and made separating from her okay.

I was like a mom with a newborn. I didn't want her out of my sight. I had never given birth, yet I had a connection to her that was so strong. I was so looking forward to having more kids. I prayed that they would look just like Ashley. It was amazing how much she looked like my husband in a beautiful girl kind of way.

I remember talking with Marc about what color eyes our child would have. Would they have green like mine or deep blue like his and Ashley's? We would talk about names and how many more kids we wanted. He always said, "I'd like one or two more," and I would say, "Well I think one to three more would be great!" It was so exciting to think about. I couldn't wait to have a pregnant belly and a life growing inside. I prayed every night that God would bless us with a child. I read pregnancy books about what to expect.

When September came, Ashley had to go to school. I remember her first day of second grade like it was yesterday. I was so sad that summer was over. Having her every day all to myself was wonderful. It helped us to bond and kept my mind off of thinking about getting pregnant. She was my little talking buddy with so many questions, and my mind was so busy answering all of her questions I didn't have time to think of my own—such as, how long is it going to take for me to get pregnant? What am I going to do with my time with no work and no child? Should I be doing something to get pregnant faster? Is it okay to work out if I'm trying to get pregnant?

These are questions that hit me hard in the coming months.

The month of September was pretty busy. Trying to get through all of the paperwork one kid brings home from school was a full-time job. Where do they get all of these trees? I felt like every time I turned around, she needed another paper signed and more

money for activities and fundraisers. She came home
with a PTO form about parent volunteers. *Perfect,* I
thought. *I will volunteer at her school till she has a
sibling. That will keep my mind off of being pregnant.*

I gave her the sheet and told her to circle the
activity she would like me to volunteer for. When
she handed the sheet back, there was fifteen things
circled! *Okay,* I thought. *I'll be busy, but they are
spaced out throughout the year. Even if I get pregnant
this month, the baby won't be born till after the school
year. I can do this. It'll be fun and give me a chance to
meet other moms.* New adult friends in this new area
might be just what the doctor ordered. So this PTO
thing would keep me busy and help me meet people.
Perfect!

Perfect till I saw all of the other moms with their
kids—plural—talking about things from years past
when all I had was the present. Perfect till other
moms found out I wasn't a "real" mom; I was "just"
a stepmom. Some mothers were so mean. One lady
was dropping her daughter off for a Girl Scout field
trip that I was helping chaperone, and she asked me,
"Is Ashley's real mom coming too?" I was polite about
it and just said that chaperoning wasn't her thing.
Another mother said, "It's so nice that you're doing
this even though you don't have any kids." I would
just say that Ashley is part my kid, though that didn't

quite cover the amount of hurt that I felt. They didn't understand that stepmoms aren't like they are in the movies. I tried to not take it personally. They didn't understand that stepparents invest real time and real love into their kids. I just prayed harder for God to make me a "real" mom and to maybe send me some "real" friends in this town.

Those months were so hard. It was supposed to be the happiest time of my life, and sometimes it was. Then there were moments that would sneak in that left me feeling empty. I had spent my entire adult life to that point in the military. I had gone on five deployments overseas. I was a supervisor. I had a purpose, and I had gotten awards and atta-boys. All until I got hurt. I now have a disk in my neck with some screws, and a shoulder that will never stop hurting and never fully work.

The military decided they would medically retire me. No longer was I the girl who drove convoys in Iraq. Now I was Jenny Cioto, stay-at-home wife and stepmom. I had no measuring stick for those two titles. No award system to tell me if I was doing okay.

Marc would tell me how happy he and Ashley were all the time, especially when I shared that I didn't know what to do. He would jokingly say that obviously I was a good cook because of the weight he had gained since we had been married. I didn't see that as a good thing (especially since he was still in the military). I tried to figure out what this stage of life was all about for me. Everything I did revolved around when I was going to get pregnant. I was ready at a moment's notice to flip some sort of switch the moment I got pregnant. I imagined myself having some sort of glow and being able to start nesting, which I heard was what pregnant women do.

I was reading a Bible study book about being a wife, and God finally hit me over the head. All those years, I found my identity in the military, and then I was trying to find my identity in being a wife. I had lost sight of where my true identity was.

Child of God.

Jesus had been with me the whole time and had never given up on me. He was patient with me when I was off in my days of convoys and traveling. He was with me when I got injured overseas and during all the mental and physical pain that I went through. He was with me when my heart broke about being retired early. Most of all, he was with me right then as I was trying to figure out how to be a great wife and stepmom.

Thank you, Jesus, for being so great to me! It is amazing how gentle He is with my hardheadedness.

So as I was jumping even further into my faith with this new revelation, I thought, *Okay, surely I was not getting pregnant because God needed me to realize where my identity was. Now that I know, I will get pregnant any day.*

I don't consider myself as a one-track mind kind of gal, but I couldn't imagine a life where children weren't a part of it. The more people told me not to think about it, the more I thought about it. Do you know how hard it is to not think about something that you want so badly? Not to mention something that people constantly ask you about. If I had a nickel for every time someone asked me if I was pregnant yet, I could have paid off my house!

It definitely didn't help that my friends were all getting pregnant just looking at their husbands. I started going down the rabbit hole of "What is wrong with me?" I lived with chronic pain from my injury, and the air force no longer wanted me. They called it retirement, but I felt rejected. Now I couldn't even get pregnant, which should be such a natural process. Why was I having so many difficulties? I started to think my body was revolting. Maybe something more was wrong—more than my injuries.

For I know the plans I have for you, declares the Lord, plans for welfare and not for evil, to give you a future and a hope.

—Jeremiah 29:11 (ESV)

3

Infertility

T his verse, Jeremiah 29:11 (ESV), is one of my all-time favorite verses. Some days it is easier to believe than others, though. Don't you agree? Isn't it funny that when things are going our way, we think, *God is great*. Then, when things don't go according to our plans, when things get derailed, we cry and ask God to fix it, for Him to put things the way we want them. Because you know the best plans for your life, right?

I always believed I was going to be a wife and a mom to a few kids. And when I got married to my husband, Marc (I was able to check off the wife part), I thought the couple of kids would happen with no trouble. We already had one (my oldest child is my daughter through marriage, no stretch marks needed, also known as a stepdaughter), so we just needed a couple more kids and a dog. Then my family would be complete.

Well, it didn't exactly happen like that. Every month after we were married was a painful and heartbreaking reminder that we were unsuccessful again and again. I started asking the women in my family about pregnancies and if they had any troubles. My mother had no issues getting pregnant with my brother and me, but it "took a little while" with my sister. She is ten years younger than me. One of my aunts had trouble. Another aunt had trouble during pregnancy. I decided it was time to go to the doctor and see if I had something to truly worry about.

So started the testing process, some very awkward and painful testing. In one of the tests, they check the tubes and see if they are working properly. I remember clearly the doctor saying, "You know, a lot of people get pregnant right after this test." I remember having all the tracking stuff ready. That month (as with every month), I was sure it was going to happen, only to find out it didn't.

They had to do several ultrasounds over the months because I had cysts on my ovaries. These cysts kept coming back, but I was told they were nothing to worry about because they didn't stick around. The doctor said, "They keep taking care of themselves."

These ultrasounds were not quite as pleasant as the ones you see on TV where the wand is going over a pregnant belly. At every test, I was hoping they would say, "Oh, just kidding. You're already pregnant."

That statement never came. To this day, it has never come. Soon after these tests, we turned to medication along with taking my temperature and tracking so many things about my body that I felt like a walking science experiment.

We finally did some genetic testing. That's when we found out that my chances of getting pregnant were low. They found that I carried two genes that were not good. One of them makes my body attack anything that could become a baby, and if a baby were to survive, I was at high risk for a stillbirth. He said it was still possible but that my chances of carrying to term were so low I might not be a good candidate even for in vitro. It was heartbreaking and lonely. I felt like I was the only one in the world who could not get pregnant.

I did not know anyone else who wanted to get pregnant and couldn't. I heard a few stories of struggles lasting a few months, but they all had happy endings. There were other stories of people not expecting to get pregnant right away, and they did. I tried being happy for all the people who told me their stories. I laughed with every person that told me, "It'll happen once you stop trying." Putting on a good front became second nature, but when I got home, I cried as if a part of me had died.

Can you imagine? My body was the problem yet again. My body was attacking any baby that tried to come along. If—when the doctor said "if," my heart sank. If I was able to carry a baby to full term, I was at high risk for a stillbirth. So any hope I had of that pregnancy glow was stomped on like a slow bug in spring. What was I gonna do?

Cry.

Cry some more.

I talked to my mother, who had found out she had the same gene but not till ages after she had all her children. I thought, *Isn't God wonderful.* My mother didn't stress about having children because she had them so young she never knew she had problems. She had three perfect children.

After crying—crying isn't the right word. After sobbing about what was going on in my body, I went through a phase of grief and sorrow. Why were my friends able to get pregnant so easily? Why was Marc's ex-wife allowed to bare his child, and I could not? Why did I have to go through this? The pity party was ugly. Oh, it was a bad kind of ugly.

I started thinking that I *deserved* to get pregnant more than so-and-so. "God, surely you don't know *their* sins. I haven't done anything nearly as bad them, and you let *them* get pregnant." It broke my heart hearing of people having abortions, and here I was *dying* to have a child. It was a dark place that I am totally ashamed of.

When you let yourself go down that dark path of self-pity and depression, it can be a hard road to bring yourself back. I prayed almost as much for a baby as I did for God to heal my grieving heart, grieving for a child that might never come.

All the while, I was hoping one morning I would wake up and just be pregnant, like it was a bad dream. It was a nightmare. The doctors had me tracking my cycle and temperature. Taking medicine. They hadn't given up the notion of me getting pregnant. They just said it would be hard, and they would take me as far as insurance and my money would take them.

Looking back, I think of myself as a shell of a person. I was so sad. I wanted it all to come easily. I wanted to be a "real" mom. I wanted to grow a cute baby with ten fingers and ten toes. I wanted strange people to come up to me and rub my unmistakable pregnant belly and ask me how far along I was, like they did to all my friends.

I couldn't understand what should come next if I wasn't going to be pregnant. What was my next step in life? What could I blame my ever-growing jeans size on if I couldn't blame it on pregnancy? Turning to food for comfort is never a good idea, especially when you don't want people to ask you if you're pregnant yet.

Comparing yourself to other people is never a good path. God made us all different for a reason. Our paths are supposed to be different. I just didn't like all of my path at the moment. After I went through the comparison phase, I went through the why phase. "Why me?"

In every phase I went through, I would pull myself out with a thought: *Maybe this is a test. Maybe I will still get pregnant and have a wonderful, healthy baby like my mom did.* No phase lasted very long. A month, a week, fleeting thoughts, then I would pull up my bootstraps and tell myself, *Someone somewhere has it worse than me. I still have hope.*

What can I say? I don't give up easily. I love my Ashley, but I wanted more children. It was that very American feeling of wanting more, only my wanting had to do with kids. I had always wanted three or four kids. Was I being ungrateful? I grew up in a culture where people can always get what they want, as long as they work for it. Well, there's no real way to work to get kids. How could this dream be smashed into a thousand pieces? In Romans 8:28 (NIV) it says, "And we know that in all things God works for the good of those who love him, who have been called according to his purpose."

I love God. I just couldn't wrap my head around how this was good. I couldn't accept that not having children was actually His will. I believe He wants good for me. How was I supposed to get through this? How was I to understand? Infertility is such a painful word. How could I go on being happy for those around me having babies with no problem? Going to another baby shower, seeing another pregnant belly. Hearing about how much so-and-so weighed, and how so-and-so is crawling, and complaints that so-and-so isn't sleeping through the night!

I wanted to scream, "I will never have a baby! Take your sleepless nights and shove them. I'd pray for a sleepless night if it meant I had a healthy baby that caused it." I was raging war inside of myself. Trying to be a supportive friend and a good Christian, but inside I was crying. I was so sad, and I tried to put on a brave face. I wasn't angry at my blessed friends, but I was jealous. I prayed for God to take all these stages of infertility from me and give me a grateful heart.

I decided to try to do as that famous phrase says: fake it till you make it. I was going to fake being happy for everyone else getting pregnant till the real feelings followed.

Slowly, I was starting to heal. My husband was sad for me, but he couldn't totally relate because he had a child. He had gone through the supportive husband role in his last marriage. He had a pregnant wife and listened to the heartbeat. He went through seeing the baby kick, birth, cutting the cord. He went through the sleepless nights and all the firsts that parents get. He went through the worried nights and calling the hospital when the newborn baby was sick. He, like everyone else in my world, could only sympathize with me. In my sadness, I was starting to get to acceptance.

I felt so, so, so alone in my struggle that most days I couldn't talk about it. Once, Ashley heard us talking about it. She was only seven or eight at the time, and her cute little freckled face couldn't have been sweeter. She pulled me aside later and told me how I always had her. She wanted a little sibling, but at least I had her. She went on to tell me that I was not like stepmoms in the movies. She told me that she told her friends I was her second mom because we love each other like "real" family. My heart broke into a million pieces again.

I love Ashley, but she had another mom that loved her too. I had to share her. I didn't like sharing her, but that was reality. Her biological mom and I got along well because we all only wanted what was best for Ashley.

I wonder how Joseph felt being the stepdad to Jesus. Talk about having to share. Wow. Huh. Not that I'm comparing my Ashley to raising Jesus by any means; I'm just talking about the ultimate stepparent situation. I wonder if Joseph had control issues, Joseph having to play second fiddle to God as Jesus's father. Joseph got to be there from the very beginning. He was there to watch Mary grow that darling baby in her belly, that baby who would save the world.

He got to be the dad but not really the dad. But then even Joseph went on to have more children with Mary.

So back to my story. I got to watch my friends' bellies grow. The looks in their eyes when they shared something about the growth, aches and pains, kicking, or even acid reflux. Then I'd watch their look go from open and sharing to questioning whether or not they were making me feel bad.

That was the worst. Some people wouldn't talk to me at all about their pregnancies, probably because they didn't want to make me feel bad. Others would over-share or make it sound horrible, like, "Trust me; this morning sickness is worse than any flu," or, "I feel so hot and gross this summer. Be glad that you don't have to deal with this yet." Which only made me want to yell at them because I would have given a kidney to experience what they were complaining about.

I guess there was no winning in any of the situations because there was an elephant in the room. No pregnant lady wants to be sad. So we just didn't talk about it. I would try to ask questions because it was the polite thing to do. Who knew—I figured maybe I would use the information someday.

I kept coming back nightly and begging God for a child. Just even one more. I would be happy with one. "I know I always asked for three, but I would settle for one, God. Please, please, pretty please, Lord. Just let me have a child. Let me tell my husband the happy news of pregnancy. Please."

At that point, we stopped trying all of the medical procedures. I went off the fertility drugs, stopped all the tracking, and took no more tests. We decided to stop trying to have a child, to see where God took us. I still hoped God would come through and I would get pregnant.

There are many examples in the Bible of women wanting to get pregnant and then not getting pregnant until long after they wanted, but inevitably they got pregnant. Just off the top of my head, I can think of Sarah, Rebekah, and Rachel's stories that are all in Genesis, and Hannah's story in 1 Samuel. I thought maybe, just maybe, those stories were meant to give those of us who struggle with fertility hope. So maybe me too? With any luck, it would happen before I was ninety (like Sarah and Abraham) because my husband didn't want to be an old dad!

My husband and I started talking about adoption. Though I was still praying to conceive, I was all for adopting a few kids. We had a four-bedroom house with only one kid. Not to mention we definitely had enough love for a thousand kids. My husband wanted to adopt two kids. We prayed for guidance and decided together to go on our crazy adoption adventure.

We looked at our options and used Google for as much information as we could get. After I found this webpage called heartgalleryofamerica.org, we looked at our state's heart gallery and decided that our best option was a local adoption agency. It was amazing and stressful, more amazing though.

I now know that God had a perfect plan for my future and for the future of our children. It wasn't the way I originally wanted. But, as my husband likes to remind me, we would never have had five kids if we hadn't gone through adoption. In our plan, we wanted one to two more. Then we would have stopped. Now, we can't imagine life without our circus of five kids.

We had to go through several classes and a background check. Then they go through a process of trying to figure out which child might fit with your family. It's a weird process of answering questions such as if you're open to boys and girls, one or the other. What ages are you thinking would fit in your family? Are you willing to take in medically complex children? Things like that. Things that you don't choose if you're having children the biological way.

After we completed the process to become adoptive parents, we got to wait. I, for one, was really tired of waiting. I know sometimes that's part of life. That didn't stop me from praying every day that the call would come. Fortunately, God had mercy on us concerning this wait time. We waited three months, which was one year after we had decided to take the adoption road.

Look after the widows and orphans.

—James 1:27 (NIV)

4

The Call

I still remember clearly when we went to our first open house for foster and adoptive parents; it was about nine months before the call. An open house is basically the first step on the road to adopt. Prospective foster and adoptive parents come to this meeting to find out the process and the realities of what it takes to adopt. They really try to encourage you and scare you there—rightfully so because we're talking about kids' lives here. If you can get scared off by just some of their stories, good or bad, you might not want to put a child into your home.

For me, the fire inside went wild! I love a challenge—bring it on. I was so excited and felt so alive I wanted to bring home a child—or twenty—that night! We went through a series of classes after that, which lasted six weeks. Some of the classes were informative, and some were heartbreaking as we learned about the reality of what kids in the foster system go through. We learned startling statistics about the sex trafficking trade and kids at risk.

I was ready to adopt forty kids when we left the classes. My husband was ready for one or two. We are definitely the perfect complement to each other. He wanted to adopt wholeheartedly too, though within the confines of our budget. His job of reeling me in from adopting a country was hard at this point, but I knew he was right. We couldn't adopt them all.

So we filled out this really in-depth questionnaire about our family and about how many child/children would be ideal, including their ages and so on. It felt weird to list out what we thought would be a good fit. I understand why they do it though, to try to make a good fit to each family.

So we decided together that a sibling group would be great. That's what we wanted. Then we had to wait. I was trying to use this time to get back into my military shape, at least a little bit. I started running and doing workout videos because I wanted to be able to keep up with having multiple kids once we got them.

Well I've never been the most graceful. I was running on the road with my dog and tripped over his leash. I fell on my good arm, and boy did it hurt. I tried to shake it off and ran back home to get some ice on it. After a week, it was still bothering me, so my husband made me go get it checked out by a doctor. Sure enough, I broke my wrist.

My husband asked, "Are you going to tell our social worker you broke your wrist?" My quick answer was, "No, I can't be the first mama to break their wrist. Besides, the cast only has to be on for four weeks. What are the chances we'll get the call in that time frame? It'll be fine. Thankfully, it doesn't even hurt that much anymore."

Two weeks later, we were laughing at the irony of my words. I will never forget *the call*. It was our social worker, and she said she had a possible match. Did you read that? *A possible match!* Oh, I was so excited I thought my heart was going to jump out of my chest and I'd never get to meet our possible match.

She went on to say it was a sibling group of three. Okay—my mind instantly did the math; that was more than two. *Okay, I can handle that. I'll have to convince my husband that he can too.* Then she said it was a newborn girl, a one-year-old girl, and a two-and-a-half-year-old boy. I was so excited I told her, "I want to say yes right now! But I need to get a hold of Marc and make sure with him first." I took down all the other information that they could give me. I do remember her telling me there were some delays because of what the kids had been through. But I wasn't concerned with that because I knew that these were the kids God had in store for us. I just knew it in my heart.

She said, "All the kids have been checked out at a hospital. The doctors could find no reason why any of the delays would be permanent. Also, this is the fourth placement for the one- and two-year-old. The current home does not want to adopt them and needs them out of her home in twenty-four hours, for personal reasons. The kids are at the point that they need an adoptive home instead of a foster home." She went on to say, "I was so excited for you when I found out that your family came up as a possible match for these kids. But it is a lot. So call your husband and talk to him, and I'll call you back in an hour."

Ah! I'm excited even writing this right now. Thinking back to that phone call and those feelings—it was all so exciting!

So I called my husband. I couldn't get a hold of him quickly enough. I just couldn't wait! He's a military cop, so they aren't by an office desk a whole lot. I had to call his dispatcher to track him down at work. Even though it was probably five minutes, it felt like forever. I finally said, "I have a question, and I need your answer to be yes!" He laughed.

I went on to tell him about our children, what they had been through, what their ages were, everything I could. Then I said, "Please! Pretty please! These are our children!"

He said, "So three? Under the age of three?"

I said, "Yes," not quite understanding why he wasn't jumping for joy!

He said, "Do you know what that means? We will have four kids. Three of them will be under three. None of the under-three are talking. You will have three in diapers."

I said, "Yes, we will!" still not quite understanding the line of questioning but going along with it. Maybe he just thought it was too good to be true.

He said, "Are you crazy?"

I said, "Yes, and I can't wait to meet them! It's gonna be an adjustment, but I think we can do it."

He started talking about what it meant to have children this young. I had babysat young children before. Plus my own sister was ten years younger, so I definitely remembered what that was like. Other than that though, I had no experience with having multiple young children. Marc wanted me to be informed. But at that point, I was already on to where they were all going to sleep and the fact that I had to buy another crib because the one we had for this call was not going to be enough. *Oh and a toddler bed. Um bottles. Do one-year-olds have bottles? I guess I should ask that. Oh and car seats—we're going to need car seats.*

We complement each other well because then he asked what the plan was. "Where is everyone going to sleep? You need to make up a complete shopping list of the things we need before they come tomorrow. And we need to redo our budget to make everything fit." My heart was pounding. I knew he was saying yes.

Then I heard him say, "Yes, if you think we can do it. Yes. Don't forget though I'm leaving in a week for one week of training for the military. I can't change that. And what are you going to do about your broken wrist? Do you know what you're getting us into?" he said with his half laugh.

I said, "Don't worry. I've got this." In retrospect, I wouldn't change a thing, but total truth here—I had no idea what I was getting myself into. My good wrist still had a cast on it. I also had some responsibilities with Ashley's school and Brownie troop in the coming months. I was going to have to find sitters or bring them with me. I thought, *Other moms can do it. I can too. I'm just going to have to do some maneuvering.* I was confident that it would all work. I just kept thanking God for delivering us children!

So the social worker called back and said, "Are you guys sure?"

I could tell there was a smile behind those words. I

said yes and thought, *What is up with that question? Four kids is not a lot. People have nineteen and make it work. I can make four work! And it will be great!*

After that, they put us in a final matching process to see if we should be the adoptive parents. *Longest couple hours of my life!* I equate it to labor pains in my own way. They called and said we were chosen, and they would be at our house at 5:00 p.m. to have us sign disclosure forms and whatnot. After that, they said that we could go with the kids' social worker to pick up the children or she could bring them to us. I elected to go with because I was so excited to meet my children. I knew I couldn't wait.

So at 11:00 a.m. the following morning, we were going from one ten-year-old to four kids. Twenty-four-hour pregnancy—who could argue with that? That night, I called my mom, who was excited to have four grandkids, and I called my in-laws and a few friends. The most common response was, "Wow." One of our friends said, "That's a lot of kids." I just told her, "It doesn't seem like a lot to me. Once we get settled into a routine, it'll be like it was meant to be." I was so excited that I would not accept anything but happiness. I knew on Facebook I would get a mixture of responses. So I chose to not put it on Facebook right away. Then we went shopping.

Oh did we go shopping. I don't think we have ever

spent that much money together ever. We needed clothes and cribs and car seats. There is no baby shower when you find out you're adopting in twenty-four hours. I could see the excitement and worry in my husband as he questioned if we could afford four kids on a military salary.

I just kept assuring him that we could and God would take care of us even if we had to cut back and clip coupons. I had a military retirement on top of his salary. I knew I could make a budget work. He sighed with relief when I spelled out the budget to him.

We were up till two in the morning putting everything together. Two cribs and one bed assembled. Then we put all new clean linen and bedding on everything. I made an old dresser into a changing table, and one of my friends brought over her changing table she no longer needed so we could have one on each floor of our house. We got a few toys and washed all the clothes we had just bought. We were a team in motion. We were talking about what we thought they might be like and how exciting it was going to be to have little ones around.

One of my husband's best-known secrets is that he's a sucker for babies. You wouldn't know it by looking at him, but he loves little babies. Then we started talking about names as we were finding homes for the influx of stuff. We decided on all three names, but we thought we would give our two-year-old son a choice of what he wanted to be called.

My husband had to work at 6:00 a.m. because the military is not so great with last-minute leave, especially before an upcoming deployment. So it really was like we were up all night with labor pains. I wanted everything to be clean for them. Pure adrenalin along with the Holy Spirit was pulling me through when I went to pick up our children.

The ride to the foster home seemed to take forever. The kids' social worker was driving, and I was in the passenger seat. I so wished Marc could come with us, but I knew he would be able to meet us at home soon after we got there. In the car, the social worker told me what she could about the background of the kids. She proceeded to tell me how "stiff" my middle daughter was because she had never really been held. I couldn't wait even more to wrap them up in my arms. I was a little nervous to have our first moments be in front of a social worker, but I kept praying for God to lead me through everything I should do.

When we got to the house, I met their present foster mom. She only spoke Spanish, so I was at a loss. I knew I should have taken Spanish instead of French in school. I was a little sad that I couldn't ask her about the kids' schedule, but then the women's twelve-year-old daughter came in and was able to translate most of the information that I wanted to know. Then she led me to a back bedroom where all my babies were kept.

I will always hold dear the first time I laid my eyes on them. The first time I got to hold them. It was great. The newborn baby, Bella, had chubby little cheeks and the cutest baby rolls I had ever seen in my life. Then I saw Tony. He was a cute little two-year-old that also had chubby cheeks and big brown eyes. He was standing in a crib, reaching out to me. Then there was Kathy. She was fourteen months and had the most beautiful brown eyes and eyelashes. They were perfect. Perfect for me. God had made these little bundles of joy for me to raise. I was sure of it.

The best part was that Tony called me "Mom." I loved it! I found out a few minutes later he called every female Mom and every male Dad. He didn't understand what those words meant because he had never known those relationships. I learned he knew four words: *mom, dad, no,* and *way*. I laughed. *Okay, at least he can talk.*

I tried to ask questions about what stages they were at. I knew Kathy was developmentally delayed, but that left a very wide range. Asking questions through the twelve-year-old daughter was a little difficult. I asked, "Is Kathy on solid food? Is she off formula?" I got back that she still needed a bottle and was on only pureed food because of not being able to chew. They were unsure of how to translate something, but I figured I would start with puree and ask my own doctor for help with how to know when she was ready for the next step. I knew most fourteen-month-olds were on finger foods, but this little girl was special. We had time to figure it out.

I asked about Tony, and she said to watch out because he didn't have a natural food shut-off when he was full. She said in broken English something like, "If you don't watch how much he eats, he will eat till he throws up." *Okay. So he likes to eat.* And she said the baby was on formula every two hours.

We went through if there were any allergies. When naps were. And I felt a little informed but not much. She was able to tell me that Kathy (the fourteen-month-old) was not sitting up on her own yet so to be careful. I had more questions, but I figured I might be better asking the pediatrician. I was so excited though. I was not going to let a little uncertainty get in my way.

On the way home, I sat in the back with the kids. I was trying to strike up a conversation with a two-and-a-half-year-old while holding my girls' hands. Such tiny hands. Such a tiny boy. I was in love. He was making lots of animated noises. I could tell he really wanted to talk.

We got them home. The social worker unloaded the three large garbage bags they came with. Most of it was dirty dishes we didn't keep and some blankets I could clean. The social worker asked if I had any questions and if I was all set. I said I was, and she left. I was able then to take a deep breath and look at my babies. They were home.

I showed Tony the toys we had bought, and then friends started dropping off things like kids' books and toy bins, anything they thought would help us with the jump in kids. My parents came with toys, outfits, shoes, and diapers. Then my in-laws came with gifts for the kids. My clean house looked like a hoarding show I had seen once. I started freaking out about the mess. I didn't want it to be a mess because I didn't want anyone to think I couldn't handle it. But I had three young, unsure babies that needed me more than the mess.

I remember thinking, *Okay, maybe I didn't know what I was getting myself into, but I still love it!*

We love because he first loved us.

—1 John 4:19

5

The Firsts

T he first weekend was a little crazy. It was just a
little more hectic than I imagined coming home
with a newborn would be. Between my husband,
Ashley, and myself, we got all the gifts and hand-me-
downs put away. We found places for kid dishes and
bottles. We organized the girls' room and Anthony's
room, all while switching off who played with who,
and don't wake the newborn.

We also had family members and friends stop by
to say hello and to meet our new little ones. It was a
happily busy time. Anthony loved all the attention. He
was an active two-and-a-half-year-old that loved all
the people around. He did not like to be told no, but I
guess what two-year-old does?

Sleep was a thing of the past. One of the badges of

parenthood is bags under your eyes. I laugh about it now, but half of the times I woke up, it was because one of the kids woke up; the other half was me waking up to check on them to make sure they were safe. The new mom in me was so excited to have a house full of kids. Yes, it was work around the clock, but I thanked God that I had this work to do.

Ashley had a soccer games on the weekend, so my in-laws came with us to give us a couple extra hands with the younger kids. Opa (my father-in-law) took Anthony on a walk around the field, and he was on a mission. He was going to teach Anthony how to say Opa by the end of the day. It was so cute.

Our family was coming together. Step by baby step, we were going to get there. I knew we had some hurdles to get through when it came to the kids' development, but I knew that my husband and I were meant to get the kids through the hurdles to come.

Kathy was (and is) so beautiful, but she was having a hard time. She was very quiet the first twenty-four hours, but then the screaming started. She screamed all the time. I heard that her and Tony's screaming was the reason the first foster home didn't work out. So it wasn't a surprise.

Kathy had had a hard life up to fourteen months, so moving wasn't coming easily to her. She had very little core muscle, so we had to do exercises with her to help strengthen them. She was so stiff. When she first came to us, it was like holding a board. Poor thing was so untrusting. She would stiffen up if you shifted your body weight while holding her. The good news though was that we got her sitting on her own in the first week. She had a long way to go, and we weren't really sure what to expect or how fast anything would come for her. The label she got at first was "developmentally delayed." Do you have any idea how broad that term is? Basically it's a label that says your child is behind, but it gives no indication as to exactly how behind or why they are behind.

My husband and I were worried for her, but that didn't stop us from going ahead with the adoption. We still loved her and were going to try to get her whatever she needed to succeed.

Kathy needed services like physical therapy, occupational therapy, and speech therapy. Thankfully, all of these people came to the house, so I didn't have to pack everyone up in the car to get to these appointments. Though I had never before been a person who loves appointments or a schedule, I found that all these things broke up the week rather nicely. Especially when Marc was away with the military.

Right before Kathy turned two, we brought her to a neurologist to hopefully get some more answers as to what was going on with her. I was really nervous because it was a couple months before the adoption was going to be legal, and we told the social worker and the biological parents about the appointment. I had hoped that the biological parents might be able to fill in some gaps with biological medical history. We knew there was no prenatal care and that she was malnourished, but we didn't have a ton of other answers.

For the appointment, because there were a lot of us, I went in with Kathy and the biological parents (bio-parents), and Marc stayed out in the waiting room with the social worker.

The neurologist had two interns too, so it was a really full room. The doctor asked a bunch of questions. I could answer all of the ones about Kathy but none about what might be hereditary. Thankfully the bio-parents were able to answer most of those.

I'm not exactly sure what I was praying for. In a situation like this, do you hope for it to be just effects from the neglect or some disease? I watched as the doctor examined my very tiny baby girl.

He then looked at me and said, " I believe all these symptoms add up to PDD-NOS. It's on the autism spectrum."

I asked him, "What does that mean for her future? Will she walk and talk?"

He just said, "I have no idea."

I left feeling a little numb and a little in denial. I had been sure it was some allergy or chromosome disorder that could be healed or treated. But autism, that's a big wide-open spectrum with a lot of unknowns.

Carrying Kathy, I went to go find Marc, holding back tears of fear about my little girl's future. I told Marc what he had said. All Marc said was, "Are you okay?"

I said, "Yes, this doesn't change how I feel about her. I'm just scared about the unknown."

A few minutes later, the bio-mom pulled me aside and said, "I'm sorry." It shocked me. I wasn't sure how to react. I wasn't sure what she was sorry about, what they had put her through or the fact that she had just gotten a diagnosis. I was guessing the diagnosis.

I just said, "It's okay." I told her that the diagnosis didn't change anything. We would still adopt all of them and keep all these precious babies together. She looked relieved.

Marc and I both teared up on the way home. To this day, he claims he doesn't remember that. We discussed that it was not going to be an easy road, but we were on the same page about going ahead with the adoption.

He predestined us for adoption to sonship through Jesus Christ, in accordance with His pleasure and will.

—Ephesians 1:5 (NIV)

6

Adoption

The day of the adoption was exciting. Our parents, in-laws, friends, and social workers were all at the courthouse. At this point, they were already ours, but now it was going to be legal. After a year of meetings, social worker visits, and court hearings, it was all going to be over. They would be ours forever. The best part was that it was also our fifth wedding anniversary.

So much had happened in those five years. Marc and I had walked through so many tears and so much joy. It seemed so surreal; it was a dream come true.

Marc joked that the three kids were my anniversary present. I told him that was fine as long as he took me out to dinner.

Everyone was so dressed up. We looked like we

were going to Easter service. The girls were so cute in their dresses, and Anthony in his little suit. Ashley was trying to get the girls to keep in a couple of hair ties, but that wasn't working out so well. We were so happy. It was perfect.

We were all waiting outside the courtroom, and I was praying that all the paperwork was in order. I had heard nightmares of the social workers forgetting paperwork and holding up adoptions.

I needed this all to be legal. I wanted this all to be set. Marc was leaving for overseas in nine days. There was no room for error. No room for delay.

He was joking that I could always adopt the kids without him, if the adoption happened while he was gone. He knew that ruffled my feathers. "Nope. Nope. Nope." I know there are plenty of military babies born while their dads are overseas, but I wanted my husband there for the adoption. I had faith that God would get all the paperwork to the courthouse and the judge would approve everything.

Well we walked into the littlest courtroom I had ever seen, and the judge seemed really laid back. I remember us all going into this little side courtroom, and he asked us what our intent was. Some of it was a blur. I know we said that we would take the children and be legally responsible for them and all that "legally responsible" meant, like financially and emotionally caring for them. There was a lot more to it, but my brain is foggy about all the verbiage used that day.

I remember everyone smiling around the table. It was great. We had to sign papers. If you've ever signed a mortgage, it was a similar amount of paperwork.

Then it was done. These three little lives that came in with a whirlwind one year prior were now ours. The way God had unfolded it all was beautiful. I could breathe.

My equivalent of labor pains was over. Marc and I were so grateful to have it all set before he had to leave. We took our whole family and all the friends that were there out to dinner. As you can imagine, there were a lot of us. It was such a happy day. I still thank God for how perfectly it happened.

Unless the Lord had given me help,
I would soon have dwelt in
the silence of death.

—*Psalm 94:17 (NIV)*

7

Not Asking for Help

Before my husband deployed, I was determined to keep doing all the things I had been doing with Ashley because I didn't want her feeling slighted. With Marc's military schedule, he was always on rotating shifts and always had to work holidays. So I was used to having to juggle the kids and activities. When he was home, we did family things. When he worked, I became a master multitasker. Then when he had to deploy for nine months, oh boy did that make things interesting.

Coleading Girl Scouts and teaching Sunday school were things that I did because Ashley had wanted me to; they were things that filled my time back when I had too much of it. When the next three kids came, these were things I didn't really want to do but felt obligated to do. I dragged the middle three kids to almost every event in the name of family unity.

Other mothers had four and were able to do it all. I was determined to be that. I knew God had blessed us with four children to take care of. So I didn't want to mess it up. I couldn't ask for help because that would insinuate that I couldn't handle it.

So many people asked if I was crazy for getting three kids at once. I didn't want them to know that, yes, it was crazy but a crazy that felt right for us. I hated how judged I felt, so I just showed that shiny, funny, sparkling side of our family.

It was hard. I felt alone. I cried alone. I couldn't ask for help because "I asked for this." It was the biggest blessing but the biggest drain on my body, mind, and soul. Do you notice all the I's? Yes, I thought I needed to do it and be supermom.

I wasn't allowed to cry that my newborn baby kept me up all night. That would mean failure. I wasn't allowed to share how scared I was at the development of my one-year-old because "I knew what I was getting into."

I had one mom ask me, "Don't you think having all these kids is unfair to Ashley?"

I could feel the anger in my face, but I didn't let it show. "No," I said. "Ashley loves being an older sister, and I've never let having a big family hold her back."

There was no doubt in my mind or heart that these kids were meant for my husband and me, and we were meant for them. Yet that didn't make it easier. It didn't make my Kathy ever stop screaming. Ever. She would hit the side of her head or bang her head on the ground and scream continuously. I brought her to the doctor once just to see if she had an earache or something of that nature. I thought maybe something was physically wrong because she couldn't talk, and she had just started crawling, but she couldn't do anything else a typical two-year-old could do. I thought maybe she had an ache somewhere.

What did the doctor say? "She is not sick. You knew that she was significantly delayed when you got her. So you knew what you were getting into."

He might as well have just slapped me across the face.

True, we knew she was delayed. True, we still said yes to this precious little girl. Wasn't it also true she was one of God's children and she needed love and help? Was I supposed to deny her because she was not ideal? I don't know about you, but for me, on Judgment Day I'm not looking at the Lord and saying, "Well, I figured since I got to pick my kids, I'd only pick the not-messed-up kids."

The fact that my daughter to this day is still delayed and ended up being diagnosed with autism among other things doesn't make me love her any less. I would never "give her back." She may never be able to say a word, but I know she loves me too and that she needs me to advocate for her.

She still needed to be helped; my knowing that she was delayed when we adopted her didn't change the fact that she needed help!

I, of course, didn't need help. Right? Because I adopted. Not only were some doctors not very kind to my questions, but some other moms weren't very nice about it either. I was trying to talk to a mom that I thought was a friend about Kathy's screaming. She just said, "You knew she was like that when you got her though, right?"

I just said, "Well, we knew she was special, but she still needs help." I didn't know what to say. Is this the same question biological moms of special-needs children deal with?

I felt like people look at adoptive parents like they should have all the answers. That it meant I should be fully equipped to deal with every situation handed to me. Maybe people think those classes we go through beforehand somehow give us magic answers. Because I adopted, I could have my house clean in a moment's notice for an adoption inspection or to host a Girl Scout party. Because I adopted, that gave me superpowers to save the world one diaper at a time!

I was drowning. Everything in my life turned into a check box. Feed the kids—check. Get the kids dressed—check. Clean the whole house—check. Get dressed myself—check. Eat—check. Tell my husband I love him—check. Tell the kids I love them—check.

I was afraid if I didn't have my list for the day, I would forget something or someone.

There was a risk of being ... imperfect.

I felt that if I wasn't perfect, that meant I didn't deserve to have my perfect family. Did that mean I shouldn't have been allowed to have kids? Are you only allowed to screw up if you give birth? It was a lot of pressure. Had I given birth to the children, then I'm sure people would have made totally different judgments.

Not asking for help led to friendships fading away. I was working so hard on how to manage the everyday that going out for coffee was a major production—one I didn't always believe I deserved because I had asked for children. Other people ask for children and get pregnant. I asked for mine though. I went through classes to be able to have my children. That means I couldn't tell people when I messed up. Or that I messed up at all.

I couldn't ask what age a kid should have a binky until because I should know. When I had questions like "When do you switch your kids off of whole milk?"

I was terrified to ask them because I thought every other mom just knew. I missed something somewhere because I dove into motherhood.

Are you getting the picture yet? Adoption came with added pressure of having it all together because I had asked for this life. It's not reality. I found that the friendships I thought I had made through my oldest daughter, other moms, were not real. They lived in a world where admitting no family is perfect didn't happen.

It took me time to absorb the situation around me and realize motherhood is messy and complicated no matter how you step into the role. Yet there were a few unkind people that said unkind words and made me believe that when one adopts, there is a stigma about it.

I remember when my husband deployed, we had only four kids at the time (yeah, ha-ha, only four), and their ages were one, two, four, and eleven. I realized then that people just say things without thinking. They feel they have the right to speak harsh words of judgment if they feel they're right.

He was gone for nine months. Within the first week, an old lady from the church we went to asked, "Why would you adopt four kids if your husband is in the military?" The things that went through my head to answer this woman weren't very Christian, so I just said, "Because I love them." And walked away. I was feeling immensely lonely because my partner through this parenting mess was going to be gone for nine months, and that's the question you ask, lady? Not "Do you need any help?" Really!

I festered on that question for the longest time. Does that mean people in the military shouldn't adopt? We shouldn't be suitable to adopt because deployment might be in the child's life? Strange. I know civilian workers that are gone from home more than my husband, but people ask *me* why I would adopt.

The question ate me up for another long stint of being afraid to ask for help. I was smart enough to know that I needed to find a great babysitter that could watch the kids once a week so that I could run errands and grocery shop and eat by myself.

We had a few babysitters that vowed never to come back. One of them was actually going to college to work with special-needs kids. I still wonder what she changed her major to after she left our house.

One day I was chatting with a mother from our Girl Scout troop about looking for a babysitter. This woman was super sweet and thought her older daughter would be a perfect fit. She was right! Finally I found a babysitter that didn't go running from my house. That time was invaluable. My regroup time.

My time to breathe and convince myself that I could go another week without asking for help.

It all hit a head around Christmas time during my husband's deployment—a little over the halfway mark of his deployment, even though it had been a rough time prior. We had a tree hit the house during a hurricane and lost power for a few days, and then at the end of October, we got hit with another storm that had us lose power for seven days.

You do the math. Seven days with no power, plus four kids (one of which is severely autistic, so she equals eleven kids when she's off routine), plus two dogs and one adult. Yep, if you said that equals disaster—ding-ding, you've won the prize.

I carried on like nothing was wrong—with my husband, who need not worry; with my kids, who need not worry; and with Facebook, which, let's face it, no one worries on Facebook. Inside though, I broke.

I decided I didn't need to be perfect and to let all my messiness out. I started to figure out where I was in the mess. A lovely group of women in my MOPS group (a Christian moms' group) helped in this process without them even knowing. They were real and messy and loving. It was great.

When I admitted that I just couldn't do Christmas because the decorating and doing a tree was more than my body could handle, they showed up at my house, fresh tree in hand, and took over! They had all our decorations out, saw my messy storage area of a basement, and still loved me. It carried my kids and me through the season. They were love.

I saw for the first time that there was non-judging moms who weren't afraid to get real. These MOPS meetings became my light at the end of a dark tunnel.

They saw us as a regular military family, not as the crazy lady that asked for four kids. They saw me as a mom in need—no judgment attached. To this day, they still probably don't know how much they meant to me. Well, unless they're reading this and saying, "Hey, that was me!" And then of course they might know. But you get the picture.

I realized I could ask for help from safe people. What a relief. I also realized that I wanted to be a safe person for others.

God is able to bless you abundantly, so that in all things at all times, having all that you need, you will abound in every good work.

—*2 Corinthians 9:8 (NIV)*

8
The Bonus Round

O ur family was complete. We had four wonderful children, and I never got to sit down. This was exactly what I had heard about motherhood.

The funniest thing though was that people kept saying that *now* I would get pregnant. Part of me wanted that to be true. I did love being a mom, and our kids were a lot of fun, but part of me wanted to get most of my kids out of diapers before we had another. That being said, *if* I found out I was pregnant, I still would have been ecstatic.

Well, right before my husband was getting ready to deploy, I was really hoping to get pregnant. This was before I knew how much struggle I'd be going through. I wanted one last chance to grow a human inside of me. I thought the timing would be perfect because he would get home right before I would give birth.

I was sad all over again when I found out that I wasn't pregnant while he was away. Marc kept telling me, "It's okay. Yes, it would have been nice, but we have four kids that keep us very busy. Plus, one of them is special needs. Don't be sad, hun."

Well, God works in mysterious ways. At the same time I was praying to get pregnant, there was a little baby boy growing in someone else's stomach.

God's plan is always better than our own. We never know why at the time, but now looking back, going through everything I did while Marc was away, it really was better off that I wasn't pregnant. It took me a long time to get to this place, but I know it's true.

About a month after my husband got back, we got a call that said a full biological sibling of our three kids had just been born, and he needed a home. Would we consider it? I, as you might have guessed, said, "Yes! I mean I think so, but I have to talk with my husband first."

My heart was racing. I thought maybe this was the baby I was praying for—wrong belly, but I had been praying for one more child. I was so excited. Bella had just turned two, Kathy was three and had just started walking, Tony was about to turn four, and Ashley was twelve. It was a good time to add our last little bundle of joy. I just had to make sure Marc felt the same way.

Can you hear the conversation? It wasn't much different from the first; only now we had a house full of kids. Despite that, I could tell he was a bit excited; my husband is a sucker for a baby, after all. But he had me go over the numbers. Could we afford another child without hurting the other four? Can you hear my answer? Yup, you guessed it. "All we need is love. The rest will work out. We have it a lot better than a lot of other countries." Yeah, I was laying it on thick. I then reworked our budget faster than it takes some people to tie their shoes.

So he asked me the plan. Yeah, he knew I had already worked out in my head where we were going to put who in what. So I told him, "We are going to move Bella (the two-year-old) into a toddler bed, give the baby her crib. Keep Kathy (the three-year-old) in a crib because she's not ready to be in a bed. Put Tony's (the four-year-old) big toys down in the playroom and have the boys in one room, the little girls in a room, and keep Ashley in her own room." I had it worked out. At least as much as I could.

Then he asked, "Do you know what you're getting yourself into?"

I hated that question. I feel like saying, "Do you

realize that I will never admit to you that I don't?" But instead I said, "Of course!"

The thing is, how does anyone know what they're getting into until they do it? I've never been pregnant, and Bella was weeks old when we got her. That was the closest I got to having a newborn in my care. So a two-day-old baby couldn't be too much harder than getting three under three at one time, right? I had a good logical train of thought. Babies don't operate on logic, but it sounded good in my head.

So there we go again. To the hospital this time, to check him out of the hospital and bring him home as if we had just had him ourselves. It was the weirdest feeling. Both of us walked into the maternity ward with an empty baby carrier. Of course my husband, being the smart aleck he is, went up to the nurse and said, "We're looking to fill this." I thought we were going to be arrested, but thankfully the nurse had a sense of humor.

The nurse showed us to the waiting room because we had arrived before the social worker. The wait was only a few minutes, but having my stomach in knots made it feel like forever. I wanted to meet him so badly.

Finally the social worker showed up, and we were led back to the nursery where he was being kept. The nurse was about to feed him, and she asked if

I wanted to feed him. I nervously but excitedly said, "Yes!"

It was amazing holding my son for the first time. He was so little yet already looked so much like his siblings it was amazing. And nerve-racking. I thought for sure the nurse was going to say that I was doing it all wrong and to give him back!

After I finished feeding him and burping this cute little boy, I made my husband buckle the baby in the carrier. There were about four women in the room besides me, all watching him strap the baby in. I felt bad for my husband having so much of an audience, but he knew what he was doing. He looked like a pro.

Have you ever gotten a sale that was too good to be true? So you walk kind of fast to get out of the store before they stop you and realize that you were undercharged? I felt like that. Leaving that hospital was a moment to remember. My husband made the joke, "Do you think an alarm will sound when we try to leave the hospital?"

I told him, "You better start running if it does."

I couldn't believe we got to drive this precious thing home! I kept praying that this was real and that we would get to keep this precious baby boy. I must confess I was a horrible backseat driver to my husband on that drive home.

I sat in the back of the van next to the baby. He

was sleeping soundly, and I just couldn't stop staring. I kept telling my husband to go the speed limit. He said, "You need to calm down. This isn't my first time driving." I kept saying, "But you're going to wake him up." None of it was meant to be mean, and thankfully my husband thought me being a nervous mom was cute.

I asked, "Do you think he's too small for the car seat?"

Marc just laughed; he knew that new parent nervousness. He still remembered bringing Ashley home from the hospital. He said, "You really need to take a couple breaths. The car seat is perfect. Yes, he's tiny, which is why the car seat has the newborn insert. He's gonna be fine. You might not be though if you don't chill out." I knew he was right, but this precious little soul was the smallest thing I'd ever had the responsibility of keeping alive.

I remember looking down at the smallest hospital wristband I had ever seen. It said "Baby Boy." I told my husband what it said. I asked him if they do that for everyone or if it was just because he didn't have a name yet. Marc told me it was because he didn't have a name.

We had decided the night before at 1:00 a.m. after three hours of going through baby books to name him Nicholas after Marc's grandfather, with a nickname of Nico. It was a name we could both agree on. Any nonfamily name either of us came up with, the other hated. Maybe it would have been different if we had nine months to talk about a name, but this was what God had given us, so that was what we named our precious baby boy.

When we got home, it was so exciting to introduce my older four to their new baby brother. It felt normal. My older ones accepted their baby brother with open arms. Literally, they all wanted to hold him. Even Bella, my two-year-old, wanted to hold him. We did the hold that so many older siblings get to do. "Ashley, if you want to hold him, you need to sit down fully on the couch."

Ashley, who was twelve going on twenty, of course said, "Why? I wont drop him."

I just said, "Take it or leave it. You need to sit down." So she did. Then Tony (who was four) wanted to. So he got the same thing; he had to sit down. I don't think I breathed the entire minute that he held Nico. It was super cute though. I took a picture that I absolutely treasure of the two of them.

We may not have had nine months to prepare each child for the adjustment that was going to be necessary. We may not have had the nine months to adjust ourselves to a change in our adult lives. But it still felt right. It was our normal. Rolling with what life throws at us is something we learned to embrace.

A gossip betrays a confidence,
But a trustworthy person keeps a secret.
—Proverbs 11:13 (NIV)

9

Their Testimonies

As a mom, I think we naturally over-share about diapers, feedings, and the wonderful and misbehaving things that our kids do. It seems normal. To answer questions people have for you *feels* normal.

Like how little Johnny stuffed a grape up his nose, and after the twelfth bath, you figured out that it was his nose that smelled. Or how little Suzie loves to streak around the house after her bath, and you have a hard time getting clothes back on that naked butt.

The problem starts when it's your family's normal but not *the* normal—when your family's normal is actually unusual. See, all my kids have another mother. That's our normal, our reality. But some of the information about how they came to call me Mom could be sensitive for my kids, like how they were not treated nicely before they came to us.

It's a tricky situation when well-meaning friends ask about birth parents and such. I am typically an open book and don't mind sharing. But my kids might. My kids all know that my belly is broken. But they don't fully understand yet where they came from and what circumstances brought them to us.

So when well-meaning friends ask, I say a broad stroke of adopting through the foster care system. I am able to tell some of their story, that they were extremely neglected, but it is not my place to go into detail. Some day if my children wish, they can find out and share that part. Because that's their story. The truth is I don't even know the whole story. It's their testimony. Not mine. And some might be put off by that, but it's the truth.

It's been complicated to know when to share and when not to, especially when I'm at a doctor's appointment for my daughter who is autistic. It's hard to tell exactly what was caused by neglect and what conditions she was born with, since autism is only one of many medical labels put on her. She also has pica, which I was told comes from malnutrition as a baby. Yet sometimes when I go over her history, I feel like it might just complicate trying to see what's wrong.

Some things that I have shared to help with

my kids' education has only bit me in the butt later because they write it in a record when I thought I was just sharing to help with the situation at hand.

In the school setting especially, I was very naive at first, thinking everyone was there for the child. But they can use the information I provide to help their own cases. Schools have a budget to think of. So I warn all adoptive parents. Before you share, ask yourself if that person really needs to know what they are asking, and is this something you want on their record?

For example, if they are asking where the birth parents came from, that's not going to help the education of your child. Don't answer such a question. In my case, the school wanted to know if they could get money from that town's education budget since the birth parents were residents there. I explained I was the mother and the birthparents had no legal, financial, or any other claim on my children, so they could not do that. I know it's different if you are fostering a child but not so if they are adopted.

Even though people seem sincere and you want to tell everyone because you're so excited, you need to control yourself. That part was hard for me. I really like to talk—understatement of the year I'm sure. I'm one that gets pulled out of church by my family because I love to talk to people.

I had one lady that was trying to see if she knew the biological family. That made me very uncomfortable. I'm not sure why she wanted to figure it out. I just gave her a funny look and pressed on.

Anyway, it becomes a gray area in the process of adoption as to what is my testimony and what is my kids'. We had to go through a year of court cases and things to make it all legal, which was a drain on my heart.

It was not terrific for me, but for my kids it was worse. They don't remember it now, but it was a constant stress until that beautiful day that they finally became legally ours!

The other tricky situation is how much to tell the kids. For our family, we didn't want adoption to be a secret because that's our child's birth story. We thought that to tell them later on that they were adopted might be worse than growing up with that as just a plain old fact. It's not something we dwell on but a fact nonetheless. Each family is different, I understand; this is just what was right for ours.

We are still maneuvering through how much to tell them about how they came to us. Anthony is at the age that he has questions. He tries to connect the dots as to how he found us. Does he need to know right now that he was in four foster homes before us? I don't know, but we tell him it's part of the path that led him to us. Does he need to know right now that no one could handle him because of all his fears and screaming? No, he can wait till he's older and can process that properly. I never want my kids to take information the wrong way. I want them to know they are loved above all else. One day they can look back at their records from the state if they want to.

All of that backstory is theirs to tell others, not mine. My kids did not have a great life before they came into our lives. It's a sad story but not their identity.

People have so many questions when they find out they're all adopted. I love sharing how to adopt. I explain what I have told you, but the rest my kids will get to choose what they share when they are older.

No matter how much background anyone chooses to share, they are our children. They still need to understand how God got them to us.

The Spirit you received brought about your adoption to sonship. And by him we cry, Abba Father. The Spirit himself testifies with our spirit that we are God's children.

—Romans 8:15–16 (NIV)

10

Love Needs No Biology

L et me paint a scene for you. I'm sitting in a
hotel lobby eating breakfast with a bunch of
acquaintances. My husband and I are away for a
weekend to attend a wedding. The topic of kids comes
up, and my husband says we have five. The woman
sitting across from me doesn't know me, but the rest
of the table knows most of our story. She says, "Wow,
you look great for having five kids." I laugh. I've heard
this before. I'm never quite sure how to take it since
I've never been pregnant. She asks the ages, and I tell
her. Then she says, "Wow, those last four are really
close. You know what causes that, right?" in a half
laugh.

I then say, "I'm not sure. A phone call?" To which
she looks baffled. My husband tells her our abridged

version of how Ashley is his daughter from his first marriage and the four youngers are all adopted.

Then in her beautiful southern accent, she says, "Bless your heart. Don't worry. Someday you'll have kids of your own."

I swear those words slapped me so hard across the face I still have a red mark. I can't even remember if I said anything back. I remember excusing myself to go get ready for the wedding.

I've heard about the story of people's births and how the moment they first laid eyes on their children, they fell in love. I've heard the stories of loving them once they were formed in their womb. I've been friends with enough pregnant women that I do get it. I am not trying to downplay your feelings or emotions. Or your special story.

So please don't downplay mine. I have my own stories. Maybe they don't involve me being in labor for twenty-four hours or pushing a watermelon out of my—but my stories are no less magical and not less important to God's plan.

Maybe your belly aches when your kids are away from you, but my heart aches when my kids are away from me. I am capable of just as much love as the next mom.

I don't believe that sharing the same DNA is what makes a mother and father love a child. There are plenty of biological parents who hurt their children that can attest to that, just as there are thousands of parents that love their nonbiological children.

When I started thinking of becoming a mom, did I think I was going to get to be pregnant? Sure I did. I thank God every day for the way he delivered my kids. Sometimes it makes me sad when someone goes on about the bond that you feel in the womb. It must be amazing to feel a little human grow inside of you. Or miserable—I've heard it both ways. But that sadness is no longer a feeling of mourning or longing. It's more like a missed experience now. I know that my family's story of how we became a family has bonded us forever.

I will never forget the first time I sat at a table with a little blonde-haired, blue-eyed girl who would someday be my stepdaughter. She was so cute and talkative. At the time, I wasn't even dating her father. We were just friends. But that little girl just made me want to wrap her up in a hug.

Getting to know her and having her be a part of our wedding was priceless. She cried because she was so happy to have two moms. She wanted me for herself. And she wanted all her friends to know I was hers.

She is sixteen now, and we are still that way. She will forever be my little one even now that she's six inches taller than me! The bond we share will never be threatened. DNA didn't build our bond; love did.

As for my middle three, I prayed for them. My husband and I went through classes. We found out on a Thursday that we had been chosen and could pick them up at 11:00 a.m. the next day. Our birthing pain was staying up all night getting cribs and beds ready, buying diapers, getting clothes. We were tired but so excited to meet these three children that would be ours. The first moment I met them in their previous foster home is forever in my memory, as I know some people's birthing stories are forever in their hearts.

I can look back and remember the exact moment I met each of the three of them. Some of the drive home was a blur. I was tired. It was a forty-five-minute drive, and I was in the back with the three of them. I had a two-year-old to hold my hand. It's a moment that is etched in my heart.

My heart still melts when I think back to my son the first time he walked into our house. Such innocence. He had been through so much in those first two years, but he was so accepting of love. It was wonderful. Not to say we didn't have our fair share of sleepless nights. Oh boy. I don't think anyone slept the first six months. I'm still not getting to sleep straight through the night, but it's gotten better.

Then the second week, Marc had to go to a military

training class that couldn't be rescheduled. One of the downfalls of adopting is you don't know when, so there is no preplanning, and there is no maternity leave. So I was on my own. I remember making a plan for each day and taking it half a day at a time. I remember thinking, *God, with your blessing, I can do this.* It had been my motto in a lot of things I'd done in my life.

Reality is I've been in some dangerous situations in my life, but the hardest role in my life by far has been becoming a mom.

God and I got really close. I was praying constantly to get me through every hour. Did I say hour? I meant minute. Maybe second. It was God's grace that got me through that time, and still His grace that gets me through today.

I got really good that week at timing. Bella had to be fed every two hours. So I would plan everyone else's meals for right after she ate. Bella would sleep as Anthony ate and I fed Kathy. I decided not to even try to potty-train Anthony till summer when he turned three and had a little bit more language. Feeding people and changing diapers mixed in with play, and lots of books became my life that week. Ashley was a huge help too. She loved reading to Anthony and teaching him new words. There was never a dull moment in our busy little house.

Then there was the first time we met our baby. I

was surprised the nursery let us in. At two days old, he seemed so fragile. We got to feed him. When it came time for us to leave, I had my husband buckle our son in the car carrier. I was so afraid to mess it up in the hospital. My husband and I both thought they would stop us at the door and say, "Just kidding. This baby isn't for you." They didn't though! The adoption worker escorted us to our car, and we were allowed to take him home! Crazy.

When we got home with him, the whole family was excited. The older four didn't get nine months to adjust to the thought of a baby brother, but they definitely accepted him with open and loving arms.

Truly I tell you, whatever you did for one of the least of these brothers and sisters of mine, you did for me.

—*Matthew 25:40 (NIV)*

11

Special Needs and Medical History

So I've mentioned that one of my daughters is special needs. Well that might be the understatement of the year, but so goes the story of struggle.

We knew when we got our beloved children there were some issues. We didn't know exactly what, but we had an almost three-year-old that said four words, a one-year-old that couldn't crawl or even sit up, and a baby who was—well a baby. So we knew that our kids needed some love.

Knowing from my painful journey of infertility that genes make up an important part of how your body works, I tried to ask as many questions as I could about their biological family.

I wasn't allowed to know everything, but the bio-parents and adoption agency did tell me a good amount because they wanted to see Kathy get as much help as she could without going through unnecessary testing if we knew something didn't run in the family.

I am so glad that I sat down with the biological parents of my kids because it helped me understand the genes part of it all. We had several meetings before we adopted where we discussed the care of the kids. Before or after the meetings, I tried to ask simple things like, "Do you know what age you started walking?" Or, "Do developmental delays run in the family?" Thankfully they didn't mind me asking simple questions. They were happy to be helpful and didn't take offense. It also helped me to understand what wasn't genetic and what may have been because of a less ideal baby life.

I was blessed that the bio-parents wanted to help. They provided me with everything they could think of off the tops of their heads. This way I could fill out the medical history according to their birth parents' history.

It's hard to have a special-needs kid/kids. It's not fun to answer all the doctors' questions, all the clinically cruddy way they ask things: "Was there any detection of problems in the womb?" "What was their prenatal care?" Or, "When did you first notice your child was delayed?" I just say, "Me, it was the day they came to me. In the span of their lives though, no one knows when they were first delayed." I borderline felt like a crappy mom when they asked about why a child wasn't nursed or how I did not know what my kid was doing at four months. I just thought, *Okay, I did tell you I adopted them, right?*

We've had to go to lots of specialists, especially for my middle daughter, throughout her whole life, and it's not ending any time soon.

She is eight years old and can't talk/communicate, go to the bathroom, or even eat on her own. It's not easy. I'm not going to sugarcoat it for you. Would I trade her in or not have adopted her if I had known all this? Nope. I wouldn't have changed a thing. Do I want her to talk? Um, yeah! It is the same as if you gave birth to a special-needs kid; it doesn't mean I think of giving her back. Parents of special needs just try to advocate the best they can for their child.

We love her. We would not trade her in for a new model. Though she may frustrate us, I love that we were able to give her a home and keep all my kids together. It means a lot.

I trust that God gives us a choice: a choice to step up to the plate or a choice to play it safe. We chose to step up to the plate. I fight for Kathy almost every day when it comes to the world or education. I have even had to "kindly" tell a woman to back off the horn when I was trying to get her off the bus.

See, Kathy has had a long struggle to do anything for herself. One thing she can do most of is get herself off the bus. I unbuckle her and grab her backpack. Then I have to tell her to get up and come on. She slowly gets herself up and makes her way to the stairs to walk down. She's a little weary of the steps, so she does one at a time and then claps for herself at the bottom. We're talking five minutes tops. I realize when you're the driver stopped behind the bus, it feels like forever, but for Kathy, it's quick. She tries. She can do it. But it takes more than the minute that cars want to stop.

I try to not let the anger of the cars on the street affect me rushing my daughter. It is hard though. I feel badly for those stopped, and I'm embarrassed when they start beeping their horn.

Yes, I admit a few times I have told the cars beeping to "Please stop! I have a special-needs daughter." I wish today's world had some compassion when it comes to being slowed down by someone.

It stinks when I see Kathy rushed around or having an aide do something for her because she is taking too long. Compassion seems hard to find in this world unless people have a full understanding of what's going on.

When it came to accepting her diagnosis of autism, did it hit us as hard as it would a biological parent? Yes, of course it did! It doesn't matter if the baby is in your belly or given through adoption, your hope is still that he/she is perfect. But did we once regret our decision to adopt? No way!

Yes, I have been asked that. Yes, I do get offended. I just say politely that it would be the same as giving back a kid that you gave birth to. Would you have chosen not to have the child? It's so offensive.

I'm not sure if people in all walks of life get asked ridiculous questions or not, but I have found that people ask the most insensitive things when they find out you adopt.

"Did you ever think about giving them back?"

"When did you know they had problems?"

"Do they know they're not yours?" Um, excuse me!

It seems to give people a license to be insensitive. As if you have any less feeling of emotion or caring involved. I have even encountered doctors that aren't nice about it, including one of our pediatricians of all people.

I had brought Kathy in for yet another ear check, probably for the hundredth time. Kathy is nonverbal, and when she goes through these bad self-abuse phases, I like to rule everything out, just to make sure she's not head banging to tell me her head hurts. It makes sense, right?

So anyway, I brought her into the doctor to get checked out, and I told him that Kathy had been really badly hitting herself and head banging. There was no fever, but I wanted to make sure nothing was wrong like an ear infection. I told him I wasn't sure what else to do to help her. Well the pediatrician proceeded to say, "Well I'm sure when you adopted her, you could tell you were going to have trouble with her."

I was floored and insulted again. Did that mean that I was supposed to leave her in the system? Did she not deserve to get adopted? Did I not deserve to get help for her because I adopted her versus giving birth to her? I really wasn't sure what was going on. I wasn't sure how to take that statement. I was sad that a doctor might think that as I was trying to get her help. Wasn't that why they took the oath and became a doctor—to help people? All I said in response was, "I just need to know if she has strep or an ear infection."

So we changed doctors, again.

Adoption is a personal thing. Just because I'm willing to talk about it doesn't mean I want you to be mean. I am open about adoption and my walk with infertility because I hope to help others. I hope maybe some other children that don't have homes can find a permanent home. There are plenty of people with love out there and plenty of children that need love.

Whether you want a special-needs child or not is between you and God. It's not an easy road, but it's a rewarding one.

He settles the childless woman in her home as a happy mother of children.

—Psalm 113:9 (NIV)

12

Mom Is a Verb

Y ou English majors out there might want to hang me for saying mom is a verb but think about it. Running is a verb because it's an action. Moms are always on the run. Serving is a verb because it's an action. Moms are always serving. Love is a verb, and moms are always loving. Even through our discipline, we are loving.

Even in Hebrews 12:6 (NIV) it says, "Because the Lord disciplines the ones he loves, and he chastens everyone he accepts as his son."

So does a mother. She cares about her children, so she teaches them, and sometimes teaching involves discipline. All of these things are actions. Mom is a name, yes, but it's a name for an action. Not just for a person but a person who does this thing called parenting. So why would we classify mom as a noun?

Some moms don't even get to be called mom depending on the relationships. Some stepmoms love the children that are in their care but are called by her first names instead of the sacred mom name. Moms come in different forms, but all are so special.

The dictionary can be a cruel place if you're on the wrong side of a scrabble board or if you're a mom that never gave birth. I mean, of course I'm a mom. Why in the world would I even look in the dictionary for the definition? I know the definition.

So why at a MOPS conference full of three thousand other moms would I even question whether or not I fit in there? Because infertility left its sting.

Infertility left its sting. It's a scar that has healed, but it left its mark on my body.

If you have ever struggled with it, whether you eventually were able to get pregnant or getting pregnant was never in your future, it still leaves a mark—a mark that the woman who carries that scar will keep forever. Some days it will be just beneath the surface, and some days the scar will be completely hidden. Yet it is always there.

One of my friends was able to conceive two children a couple years apart, both through IVF. Their story has a happy ending, with two perfect little girls.

And still years later, my friend saves a picture of her daughter at five cells old.

Can you imagine? Five cells. Most women have no idea that they are pregnant at that point. Some mothers don't even care. But because of this friend's struggle, not only is she able to have a picture of her daughter at five cells old, but she cherishes it!

What a blessing to have that memory and to have that gratefulness. If she didn't have that struggle, she would have never known the exact blessing that God had in store for her.

Other women's scars may not have the same outcome. I have a happy ending as the result of my struggle with infertility, but the infertility part was never healed.

Some moms can't even be in the room while childbirth is being discussed because the wound is so great. Other women have lost a child at birth. Some even feel judged because they had a baby, but they had to deliver via C-section. I know it shouldn't, but it really shocks me how judgmental women can be.

My heart breaks when someone confides that having a C-section was hard for them because of the judgment that happened after. My friend's family was all for a natural birth. She was concerned some might think less of her because she had to have an emergency C-section. I said, "Don't worry and just be grateful for your little bundle of joy." Moms have no time to carry guilt about such things.

Thankfully, my faith helped pull me out of the pit of depression about infertility. Then and only then was I able to say yes to adoption.

Adoption is not for the faint of heart. The struggles of motherhood will not heal the sadness of infertility. Adoption is something you come to when you are okay with whatever God has in store for you.

Motherhood requires all of you. It is the biggest action a woman can do. Whether you stay at home or work, motherhood uses brain cells and heartstrings you will never understand until you have a child that is given to you to take care of. A child that is dependent on you for providing all of its basic needs along with all of the love, teaching, and patience you can possibly provide.

Anyway, circling back to the conference. You may be thinking that I am crazy for even wondering if I would be accepted (because I have five children, after all), but so many people I've met have been taken off guard about my path to motherhood.

That may seem ludicrous, but society often judges things that are outside of the norm. The society we live in has many opinions on both sides of the fence. It does seem like a lot of people that are normally nice feel that they can be cruel on the Internet and it's okay. People judge and publish harsh words without realizing or caring who is on the other side.

The other side always believes the opposition is way out of whack. Well, can't we all be right? Is the true answer somewhere in the middle? Yes, it is. The definition you believe is right depends on your life experiences. So if this answer is subjective, then how do we get the truth? Well, the quick answer is it's all true. God gave us all unique circumstances so we could help each other out, not tear each other down.

The long answer is it's whatever works for you and your family. If you were a parent that gave up your child because you knew you were not going to raise the child you gave birth to, then that's right for you. To you, the adoptive mom may always be the adoptive mom. If you are the child, most likely the adoptive mom is just called mom, and it's the bio-mom that has an added word. Whatever the case, when it comes to the relationship a mom has with her child, I do not believe it matters whether she gave birth or what her label actually is. Being a mom is an action, a relationship. It's a living, breathing, vulnerable relationship that goes far beyond biology.

Being a mom doesn't depend on if you delivered naturally, using an epidural, by C-section, using a surrogate, or by adoption. The dictionary cannot sum up what goes on to make a woman a mom.

It is far beyond what words could explain, though you know I had to try. I ask that we all breathe acceptance and love.

Since God had planned something better for us so that only together with us would they be made perfect.

—Hebrews 11:40 (NIV)

13

Thanking God for His Plan

W e all have a plan for our lives. From a wee child, we are asked what sport we want to play, what we *want* to be when we grow up, where we want to live, and so on. Though if you've lived past five, usually you realize that what you have planned and what is in store for you can be two completely different things.

The trick of it all is to be able to cope with the changes when your plan does change—because it will. I don't know of one person where everything happened in their life exactly the way they planned it to go. So we have to learn to deal with the change. For some people, dealing with life change happens easily. For others, having their life change can be hard.

I am not always good at change that I did not okay. I don't process it well. Usually I have to mull something around in my brain a bit and adapt it as my own before I'm okay with any sort of change.

Sad to say, I did not come to this amazing revelation on my own. An old supervisor in the military told me that once, when I was being very opinionated about changing the location of my desk. It was a stupid desk change that ended up better in the end. But that didn't stop me from initially fighting to not have the change.

When the supervisor suggested that I was just opposing the change because it was a change, I got *very* defensive. I did not want to believe that I could be such a person. No, the person he described was hardheaded and stubborn. I was *not*. How dare he believe I didn't like change?

Then I took a step back. I looked at the situation for what it was. Why did I honestly have a problem with this desk change? Did it affect my work or my pay? No and no, so why then did I immediately jump in with my objections instead of thinking it over?

Do you see where this is going? Yeah, I wasn't too happy with myself or the truth my supervisor had just spoken into my life. So why did I immediately object?

I'll give you the reason: because it didn't come from me, it was a change that I was not prepared for. I wanted to be in charge of where my desk was. If you've ever been in the military, you realize that your life is not your own. Where have we heard that before? Oh yeah, the Bible. We are not in control; God is. Such a curse it is to want to be in control of every move and then realizing that you're not even in control of where you sit!

Having spent ten years in the military, you would have thought that what the Bible preaches about handing over your control to God would have come more naturally to me. Now that's a good laugh.

I struggled every second when my plan of getting pregnant my first year of marriage didn't work. I pained. I asked why. I did not want to "just leave it up to God." I didn't want to not worry about it. I wanted it to happen!

People kept telling me, "Stop worrying about it, and it will just happen." Well maybe that works for some people, but I knew that statement was not going to be true for me.

My brain could not wrap around the idea at first that my plan was not the same plan that God had in store for me. I thought I had the best plan for my life, so why wasn't it happening? Why wasn't God listening?

The answer is simple, my friend: Gods plan was far better and far greater than I could have ever imagined. I needed to become less. He needed to become more. Just like that famous country song, "Jesus, Take the Wheel," I needed Jesus to take the wheel to my life and lead me to where I was supposed to be.

When this journey began, I still thought I had control of my life. I had in my head the perfect plan for my life. The white picket fence and the perfect children with a perfect husband. It was all going to be magnificent, just the way I planned it.

Well, my story has some heartbreak in it. There is struggle, yet those times I see now as completely necessary. I needed to be humbled. I needed that heartbreak so that my image of what life should look like could be shattered. In that brokenness was the only way that I could say, "Whatever you want my life to be, Lord."

That place of realizing I wasn't in control and that I could change my plan was where He needed to bring me, so that I could be open to another version of my life story. I needed to be open to my life changing drastically overnight.

Behold, His plan was so much better. My not-so-typical family is the most perfect plan. My wildest make-believe story as a child would never have come up with this beautiful, messy, and wonderfully perfect story of my life. How amazing is it that God can use everything for His glory and His goodness? Some days I just have to pinch myself and say, "Yes, this is real!" Other days, I say, "God, are you sure about this?" But most days I just say, "Thank you."

Let no debt remain outstanding, except the continuing debt to love one another, for whoever loves others has fulfilled the law.

—*Romans 13:8 (NIV)*